D1310914

Preface

Concealed beneath a garden in a suburban back yard, a miracle is revealed. Experience the journey of a caterpillar as he undergoes nature's little miracle of complete metamorphosis of an egg into a caterpillar into a chrysalis into a shiny butterfly!

The many exciting details of a butterfly's life cycle are brought to life with rhythmic writing style, imaginative illustrations, and vivid colors – tapping into children's natural sense of wonder and discovery (grownups too!) – all composed in a book to help make learning science fun for children.

Acknowledgments

Thanks to my amazing wife, Carol, and astonishing daughter, Samantha, for their wonderful support and always cheering me on.

Thanks to my copy editors, Dave Leong and Anita Rodriguez, for fine-tuning the structure, tone and voice – ensuring the consistency and creative flow of the book.

Thanks to Tom Turpin, Purdue University Professor of Entomology – Retired, for double-checking the scientific facts to ensure accuracy.

Copyright © 2019 Steven King
All rights reserved. Printed in the United States of America.

ISBN-978-0-578-50394-3

No part of this book may be used or reproduced in any form or by any electronic or mechanical means, including information storage and retrieval systems, without permission in writing from the publisher, except by reviewers, who may qoute brief passages in a review.

Written and illustrated by Steven King
Visit themetamorphasisbook.com

Have you ever Met a Morphosis?

Written & Illustrated by
Steven King

In our own backyard right under our noses,
in a tree Mom planted or on top of her roses,
there is a world of insects that transform as they grow,
some develop quickly and some are slow.
A butterfly's life cycle is a perfect example of this;
it's a wonderful process you don't want to miss.

The life of a butterfly goes through four stages;
a complete change in shape takes place as it ages.
Stage one has begun in the plants as they sway,
on top of a leaf a tiny egg lay.

5

Even though the egg is innocent and small,
within its shell is enough magic for all.
In a few short days the egg stirs about,
a larva inside chews his way out!

What excitement, amazement and disbelief,
a teeny tiny caterpillar steps out on the leaf.
With a huge appetite stage two begins,
a series of eating and shedding his skins.

Voraciously hungry, he heads straight for a tree,
he swiftly crawls to a leaf to start his eating spree.

The very next day is no different than the last,
as he eats every leaf so incredibly fast.
Eat, eat, eat is all he will do,
bite, chomp, munch, CHEW, CHEW, CHEW!

Chewing up all those leaves is sure to make him pop.
The caterpillar has an appetite that just won't stop!

All that eating makes him grow quite a bit;
his skin is too tight and will no longer fit.
Inside his body is a new layer of skin,
ready to come out that has been growing within.

He wiggles and pushes to get out of his skin.
Relieved from the pressure, he sports a grin.

Shedding his skin is all part of the show.
It's a process called moulting that allows him to grow.

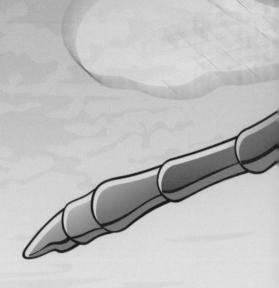

With his old skin off and unmistakably bigger,
he's ready to eat again with excitement and vigor.

He repeats this cycle through the day and the night,
and continues to grow as he takes every bite.
As he steadily grazes like an eating machine,
he will shed a few times through his growing routine.
The last moult happens in the second week.
It's not like the others, it's very unique!

Ready to shed his skin one last time,
he carefully searches for a branch he can climb.
He creates a silk button he connects himself to,
twisting while hanging secures him like glue.

Attached to the branch he wiggles about,
an exciting new form is on its way out.

Shedding and hanging is difficult to do;
the skin splits open and unveils something new.
A chrysalis is revealed as it dangles from the tree.
The caterpillar has become a pupa in stage three.

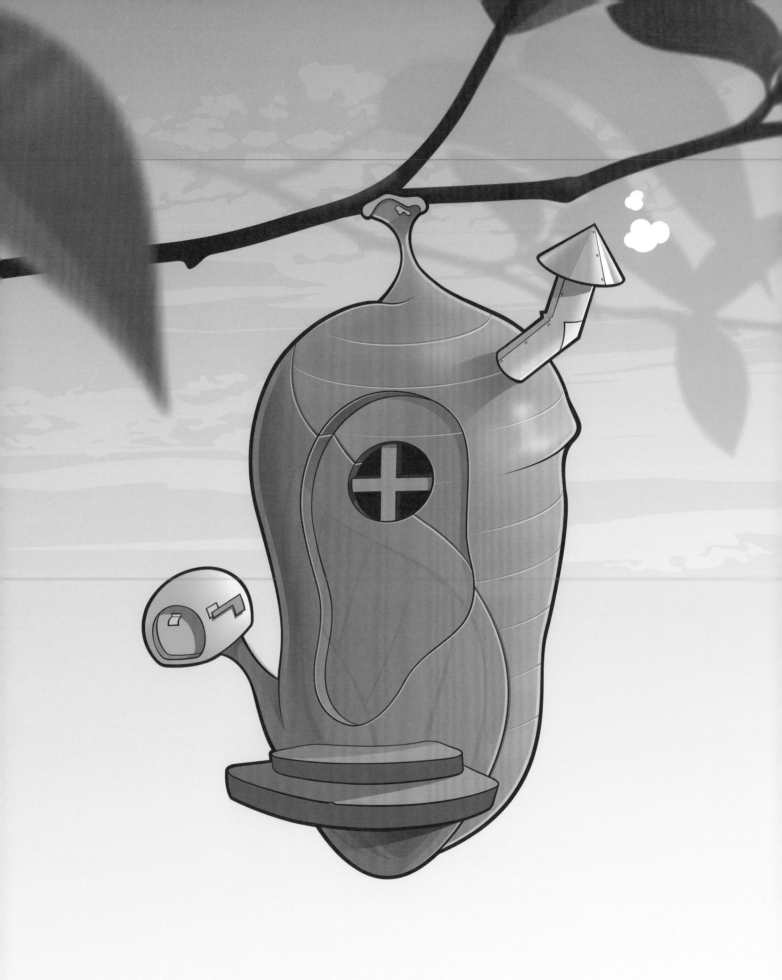

The chrysalis hardens to create a protective case.
There's not much room in the tiny little space.
Inside is the making of amazing new things,
rebuilding body parts and forming some wings!
After two weeks, he's ready to sprout,
pushing and stirring to **force his way out!**

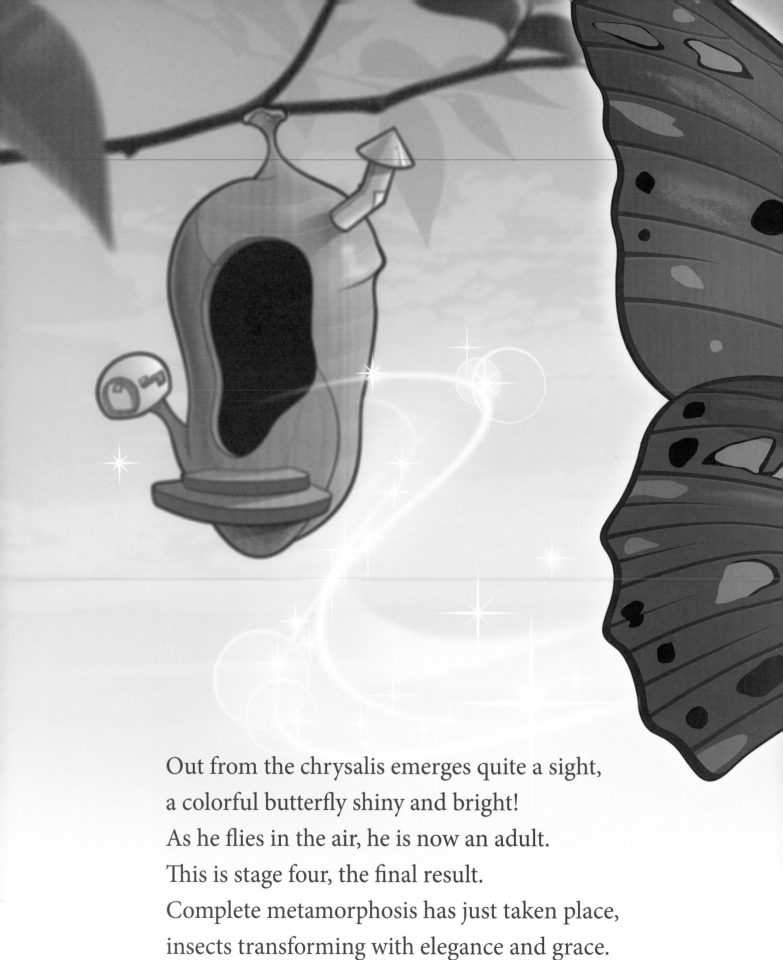

Out from the chrysalis emerges quite a sight,
a colorful butterfly shiny and bright!
As he flies in the air, he is now an adult.
This is stage four, the final result.
Complete metamorphosis has just taken place,
insects transforming with elegance and grace.

GLOSSARY

Butterfly: Flying insects with two pairs of wings, a proboscis, clubbed antennae, slender body, and large, broad, often conspicuously marked wings.

Caterpillar: The common name for the larvae of members of the order Lepidoptera (the insect order comprising butterflies and moths).

Chrysalis: Butterfly at the stage of growth when it is turning into an adult and is enclosed in a hard case. The hardened outer protective layer of a pupa.

Instar: An insect is called an instar when it is between two molts. A newly hatched insect is called a first instar or larva. An adult is a final instar. Most caterpillars (butterfly and moth larva) have five or six instars.

Larva: A larva is a distinct juvenile form many animals undergo before metamorphosis into adults.

Life cycle: Butterflies go through four different life stages: the egg, larva (caterpillar), pupa, and adult.

Metamorphosis: The process of transformation from an immature form to an adult form in two or more distinct stages.

Moult: The shedding of old feathers, hair, or skin, or an old shell, to make way for a new growth.

Nectar: Nectar is the sweet liquid produced by many flowers. Adult butterflies sip nectar through their proboscis.

Proboscis: A a tube-like, flexible "tongue" that butterflies and moths use to sip their liquid food (usually flower nectar or the liquid from rotting fruits).

Pupa: The stage in a butterfly's life when it is encased in a chrysalis and undergoing metomorphasis.